Walking

in the

Spirit

Geraldine Cooper

Ampelos Press

Dedication

To our daughter, Sheryl,
who the Lord was able to use
to meet many of our needs
and to all our family.
We love you!

Contents

Preface

My husband and I were saved and filled with the Spirit when we were in our forties. Most of this book is from over twenty years ago. We are in our eighties now and still walking with the Lord, but we move a little slower.

Jerry Sr. is eighty-seven now, but when he was still working, he received the factories' President's Award for the volunteer work we did in hospitals, prisons, and senior citizen homes. He received an eagle from the company to represent the award. We started when our children were teenagers. They were saved first.

We now have grandchildren, great grandchildren, and great great grandchildren. We just celebrated our sixty-fifth anniversary.

My favorite Scripture, which God said to memorize, is Psalm 91.

1

The Wise Man Builds
His House Upon a Rock

We lived out in the country in a farmhouse with an open field in back of it. Many times, I would take my Bible and my blanket and just go into the field under the pretty blue sky and talk to the Lord. I'd ask what He would have me read, and He would give me a Scripture to memorize.

Two of the first ones were Isaiah 53:4, "Surely he hath borne our griefs," and Isaiah 53:5, "and with his stripes we are healed." Then, when I was in a Bible study or prayer meeting and someone asked for prayer for someone who was ill, the Lord would tell me to pray for that person and pray the Word He had taught me that week. It was a beautiful way to learn how to pray.

Daily He took me to Scriptures, and then He would send someone who needed that certain prayer. I remember the Scripture in Exodus 23:26 which tells us God doesn't want anything or anyone to cast their young or be barren. The week I learned that Scripture, a saleslady came to my door. She was new on the job. We got to sharing about Jesus Christ and what the Bible says, and then out of the clear she said to me, "I've had five miscarriages. Do you think the Lord is trying to tell me not to have any more children?" I was then able to give her the Scripture that the Lord had taught me. I prayed with her a few times, and about a year later she had a baby girl! But that's getting ahead of my story.

--·�֎·--

Over the years we lived in our farmhouse, we always had relatives living with us. It was there that our family found the Lord. My children had become "born-again," and my husband started to read the Bible just to defend himself. One day he asked our son, Jerry, a question about the Bible. Jerry said, "I don't know the answer, Dad, but God will show you." In the background we had a Christian radio station on. The announcer was giving the answer to that very same question! It wasn't very long after that my husband accepted Jesus also.

Soon after that, one of my neighbors came to know the Lord. We would sit together and watch a Christian TV show. When the host said, "Let's pray," we would kneel together and hold hands and pray. That's where I first prayed late one night and asked Jesus Christ into my life. I didn't even know what I had done until about six months later when my son started going to a home Bible study. He shared with me and got me to watch this same TV show again.

I wasn't in any group at this time, so I just prayed and asked the Lord to show me what I needed to know. As I asked questions, the answers began to come one after another. I didn't have any problem with talking to the Lord and hearing from Him. I accepted it as the normal part of every born-again person's life. I had so much joy that I believe I smiled continually for six months straight. My cheeks actually hurt from smiling so much!

-·❋·-

Two weeks after I started watching Christian television again, my son brought home a book on speaking in tongues. I read it and opened my mouth and started speaking in tongues. My husband was in the shower. I wanted him to hear, so I just kept right on speaking until he came out. I could tell how happy he was for me. The next day I sang all day in my new language. My husband knew it was different since I sang better than I ever had.

It wasn't until a few years later, when I was at a meeting, that the Holy Spirit moved me to give a message in tongues (1 Cor. 12:10). It was a small group. I always thought I knew what I was speaking, but the speaker there confirmed I had just given a message in Spanish, and he was able to understand some of it. Another woman there later told me that she had asked the Lord for someone to give a message in Spanish. So, again it was confirmed.

-·�֎·-

Getting back to our farmhouse, I started walking daily in the Holy Spirit. Most of the things that I did, I would have been doing anyway, but now it was in God's timing.

We had many dinner guests and began witnessing to our families. We soon learned to let our lights shine and keep our mouths closed until the Holy Spirit had them prepared.

My husband and I began to read constantly and to listen to some very good teachings. We found out that Jesus not only died for our salvation, but that same day

He provided everything we would ever need (Isa. 53:4-5). We started in a day-to-day walk with the Lord.

We felt we were to build a home on the land that we had, so we made plans to put in a long drive to the back. We measured things out according to the ordinances that we had to follow. Our home is now built on the very spot where I sat and talked to the Lord. (He sure knows how to bless us!)

We had house plans and went to a Christian builder. He took us to a bank where the president was a born-again believer. He said they prayed about their loans. We talked about the Lord for forty-five minutes and filled papers out in fifteen. What a blessing!

At this time, our children were still in school. That was six years ago. Since then, there have been graduations, weddings, two more homes, and grandchildren.

After getting married, our children moved in with us to save for a home. Young Jerry and his wife were first.

The Lord had shown my husband that he was to divide the land for the children. When it was surveyed, there was enough to meet the requirements for two more homes, except for one thing—we didn't have enough road frontage.

We had to attend a meeting to talk about putting in a road. Right before we went, we prayed, and the Lord gave me a Scripture: "I am come that they might have life, and that they might have it more abundantly" (John 10:10). We felt nothing was going our way until we heard someone there saying loud and clear, "ten-ten." We knew God had everything in control. It was decided we had to put in a road. Jerry and his wife started building their home.

After about nine months, our daughter, Sheryl, called to say that she and our son-in-law would be moving in soon to start to build their home. There would be three of them moving out. So, before long, we had six people (almost seven), three dogs, one cat, and a goldfish living together.

These are days that I thank God for because they are treasured memories for me. Only with God's guidance was I able to keep my old self from interfering. I learned to look up Scriptures that pertained to me, my family, and different situations and to speak them out, calling things that were not as though they were (Rom. 4:17). What a great way to live.

-·⁂·-

Women, what a challenge! If you think it's dull being a housewife, mother, or grandmother, call me and let's talk.

What a difference prayer can make in our lives! We have such liberty in Jesus Christ that we can know where our direction lies. If we are open, God shows us how to pray for our families even before we know their needs. We can go on what the Word says, not on what we feel or what others are going through. Praise God!

2

Go Thee Therefore . . . And These Signs Shall Follow

When we first moved into our new home, I was working in a local inn as a maid. My job was cleaning and making beds. I prayed as I went about cleaning and learned to listen to God's direction. I prayed every day that I would do God's will for me.

One night while asleep at home, I suddenly woke up and turned to see our clock. I noticed the time was 2:22. Another night, I was up in bed, not knowing what woke me, and again the clock said 2:22.

That week as I was cleaning the bathroom in one of my rooms at the inn, there was a piece of paper left on the counter. I went to throw it away, but I decided I had better look at it first. On it was the name and telephone number of a local born-again minister. For the first time, I heard the audible voice of the Lord say, "This is what I've been showing you." I looked up and back over my shoulder, but I didn't see anyone. I was in Room 222.

I still didn't know what I was supposed to do, so I just waited on the Lord to show me. Then, one day as I was cleaning, someone asked me for an extra blanket. He said there was a sick person in Room 222. Believe me, I prayed hard that afternoon to see what I was to do. It came time to go home, and I knew I couldn't leave without praying for this sick person. Then I thought about the paper with the name of the minister on it.

I went into Room 222 and very quickly asked a man who was in bed if he was a born-again Christian. He replied, "Yes." What a relief! I told him I knew the minister whose name was on a piece of paper in his room, and I asked if I could call him to come and pray. He said yes!

As I walked to the phone, I remember reaching over and touching him on the shoulder. I felt what Jesus describes in Luke 8:46 as virtue leaving. I called the minister, and he was there within a very short time. I then left for home.

The next day as I was cleaning, I noticed the man was no longer sick in bed. The devil hit me with the thought that I had really done a stupid thing. I remember saying to the Lord, "I feel real stupid, but I did what You were telling me to do." I didn't hear anything about it from anyone all day, and I went home wondering what had happened.

That night, I went to my regular Bible study, and there was the man. He gave his testimony on how he thought he was dying. He said when he looked up and saw me, he thought I was an angel. That very night he was feeling much better, and the next day he was able to go to work. Praise the Lord! After that I was more open to the Lord's direction.

--�֎·--

One time as I was cleaning, I felt the Lord was telling me about love. I said, "Lord, what are You trying to teach me?"

The next day as I was cleaning a room, I saw a Bible on the table. Written all around the edge was the word "Love." I opened the cover to find that it belonged to a man by the name of Love. I went home and shared with my husband what I had seen. He agreed that we should call him and ask him to come to our Bible study. (By this time, my husband was going every week too.)

I called Mr. Love and again started with, "Are you a born-again Christian?" I felt since the Lord was leading, we had to have that in common. He said yes.

We picked him up and introduced ourselves. After we got to the study, he shared with everyone how he had been a minister on death row during the riots in Oklahoma. It's been a few years now since we talked, but the last I heard he was preaching over the radio there. He also had a beautiful talent of painting birds.

-·※·-

I have another testimony, which I was going to tell, about a man looking for something in South America, but I feel I'm supposed to wait and tell this another time.

-·※·-

One day as we were on our way to a baseball game to watch our son's team play, we passed a counseling center that was run by the state. The Lord said He wanted me to go in. Sometimes it takes a little longer for that boldness that the Lord supplies to come upon us. So, I prayed and said, "Lord, I'm willing, but my flesh is weak. Help me!"

About two months later, we were in the same situation (on our way to a game at the same place), and the Lord spoke to me again about going in. I drove around the block, prayed again, and kept saying, "I'm willing, Lord. I'm willing." Then I parked the car and went in.

There was no one inside that I could see, and then I heard someone coming down the stairway. It was a young lady. Not knowing what to say except that I knew the only reason I was there was because the Lord had directed me, I used that same question again. "Are you a born-again Christian?"

She looked at me sort of surprised and said, "Yes, I am."

I then shared with her how I got there and asked if she needed prayer for an illness or knew of someone who did. She said she was going on vacation the next day and planned to visit a sister who was sick.

I talked to her for a while and found out that she was married to a young man who was originally from my hometown. He had relatives on the same street where I lived while growing up.

It wasn't until about six months later, the night before my daughter, Sheryl's, wedding, that she called to tell me that the sister had been healed and would I pray for someone else. I thought of the Scripture, "Love thy neighbor as thyself" (Matt. 22:39). We don't always know where we'll find a neighbor.

The Word says that daily the Lord looks for someone to stand in the gap (Ezek. 22:30). We need to know how many times we are that person. Sometimes, as the Word says, He can find no one.

-·⁂·-

On this one occasion, the Lord told me to get a job as a census worker. I was to volunteer. Did you ever try to volunteer for a paying job? I was told I couldn't do that! I had to be paid.

I was a little uneasy at first, but the Lord knows everything about us. The very first house I went to turned out to be the house of a dear old lady I had gone to many Bible studies with. So, I received a blessing at the house of the first person I talked to. This really encouraged me.

Everything went very well for me. I could see the Lord preparing the way, even providing a few mailmen who took time to answer my questions and give me directions.

There was one little old lady almost waiting for me to get there. I shared with her that I was born-again. Someone else had already sown the seed. I asked her if she wanted to ask Jesus into her heart, and she immediately said yes. After we prayed, she said, "Now I can call my friend and tell her that I got it too!" What a blessing!

-·⁂·-

The Lord had me visit people in my neighborhood. Sometimes just to sit and talk; sometimes to help out with whatever I could. After sharing Jesus with them, they were ready to ask Him into their hearts.

On one occasion, the Lord told me to have a Bible study in my home. The very first day, my new neighbor asked Jesus into her heart. Many times, I have seen how our Lord cares for just one person in the things I have done and the places I have been sent just for one person.

One time we had a few ladies in our home for lunch. My husband and I decided we would not witness but just show our love. I can't even remember what was said, but all of a sudden, one of the women said to me, "I just want to be saved. How can I be saved?" She said that about three times!

I was stunned at first, but then I quickly said, "I know how. Pray with me." And she did! So, I leave it up to the Lord to plan things differently from what we expect!

-·⁂·-

Going back to the Lord looking for one person to stand in the gap, we were at a healing service that Oral Roberts had in Philadelphia. The week before, there had been another evangelist there. A man sat by the escalator selling pencils.

I could feel boldness that comes after being in such an anointed service. I walked up to this man and asked him if he knew Jesus. He said, "I'm not saved." I said something else, and again he said he wasn't saved. I then asked him if he would pray and ask Jesus into his heart, and he did.

My husband said later that he thought it was silly for me to stop and ask him that question after thousands of people had passed by. He was really surprised to hear he had not prayed with anyone else. He was waiting to be asked.

-·�֍·-

One time while just being open to the Lord, He told me that I was to get up at five a.m. and pray in tongues for one hour each day. At this same time, I had started to read a book that a friend had given to me. She had given it to me a year before. As she handed it to me, the Lord told me to put it away for a year. Now I was told by the Lord to start reading it the week before. It showed me different ways of praying.

About the fourth morning of getting up to pray, I was sitting at my dining room table praying in tongues when I saw in a vision a large explosion that took the shape of a mushroom. At first, I became upset, but I realized that I was in prayer. "Okay, Lord," I said. "I see what You're showing me. Now what shall I pray?"

He brought to mind one of the prayers that I had just read in this book and told me to pray that prayer. I did.

A few days later, I had the news on as I was driving. I heard the man say there had been an explosion in Philadelphia in a chemical plant. I didn't think anything about it until he said that it took the shape of a mushroom up in the air and that it was a miracle no one was hurt! Praise God!

3

He Gives His Angels Charge Over Us

God shows us may things in many different ways. Many times, both in the spirit and in person, I have seen angels sent to help me and others.

--·✳·--

My mom lived in a little town in upstate Pennsylvania. I had told her that if she ever needed me, I could get a bus on a Thursday morning. (My grandmother lived with her, and she sometimes needed help.)

One week, Mom called and asked if I could come. While on the bus, I prayed and read my Bible.

The bus driver left us off in front of the station. I wasn't really looking where I was going. As I reached to open a door to a building, I saw a hand there. An elderly man said to me, "You're going in the wrong door."

I looked up and saw that I was and thanked him as I walked away. He had such a nice smile on his face. As I walked to the bus station, I felt I should look back, and there was this same man smiling at me. I thought to myself, *How did he know where I was going?* I then got busy getting a ride home to Mom's.

That night, as everyone got settled into bed, I opened my Bible. I thought about the events of the day and the smile on this little old man's face. I said, "Lord, who was that man? How did he know I was going in the wrong door?"

I looked down at my Bible, and there, opened before me, was the Scripture in Hebrews 13:2: "Be not forgetful to entertain strangers: for thereby some have entertained angels unawares."

-·✳·-

Another time, my son, Jerry, and I were going to the airport to see his fiancée and family off for England. They were already at the airport. We were late and called so she would know we were on our way. We reached the desk and asked them to give a message for us. Racing through the terminal, we got there just in time to see the plane taking off into the sky. We waved, hoping they would see us.

It was the overseas terminal, and it was quite empty except for a few workers. But there was a man with a beard and a black hat and coat who looked like a rabbi. He turned and said to us, "There was a family on the plane that was waiting for someone. They tried to hold the plane as long as they could, but they had to go."

We thanked him and started to leave when I felt an urge to look back. He was nowhere in sight. As we were driving home, I said to Jerry, "Wasn't that nice that the man there was able to tell us so much." Again, I received Hebrews 13:2, "Be not forgetful to entertain strangers: for thereby some have entertained angels unawares."

-·�֍·-

One day, as my daughter, Sheryl, and I were going shopping, my eyes were opened to see angels sitting on my car. There were five of them. They said they were there to protect me. We spent most of the day shopping. When we came out of the center, it was dark and snowing. I asked Sheryl, "Which way should we go? How are the roads?"

Sheryl answered, "What difference does it make?"

I knew instantly that the Lord was speaking through her, for I then remembered the angels that God had shown me on the car that morning. Just being reminded of that made me relax and ask God which way we should go. We headed for home with no problems.

-- ❋ --

Once in a while, when the Lord leads me to an evening Bible study without my husband, He sends a special angel along with the angels that are outside the car. This one sits beside me, and the Lord allows me to see him. What a blessing!

I have been at many meetings where I have seen ministering angels. Sometimes someone will pray to send them out to someone, and I see some leave. They are different sizes and dressed in different kinds of clothing.

-- ❋ --

Having our spiritual eyes opened also allows us to see evil spirits that are present. I have been at deliverances where I have seen demons leave. Sometimes they have even made faces at me as I saw them leave.

One time, while at a meeting and praying with the group for our nation, I saw a demon with bright red hair, a steel hat with horns, and a weapon on his side hanging down from a belt. I knew somehow spiritually that he was a spirit of assassination. As I came against him, I saw two warrior angels, armor and all, come get him and back him out the window and away.

After this had happened, one day I was with a friend and her daughter. We were sitting and talking. The daughter kept saying, "Let's pray."

After a few minutes, I said, "Barbara, let's pray and see what the Lord is trying to show us." We prayed for our nation and president about two hours before someone tried to shoot him. So, when the eyes of my spirit were opened to see this demon (assassination), I wasn't surprised.

-·✳·-

One evening, while watching TV, the preacher called for ministering angels to walk through the audience and touch people. With my spiritual eyes opened, I saw a hand reaching out and touching a woman in a wheelchair. I pointed her out to my husband and said that an angel had just touched that woman. At the same time, the preacher asked for those who received a touch to stand up. She got up out of her wheelchair! God is so good!

-·✳·-

Even as I am writing this now, a few years later, a minister on TV is talking about angels. Second Kings 6:17 tells us that Elisha prayed, "O, Lord . . . open his eyes that he may see!" The Lord opened the eyes of Elisha's servant. When the young man looked, behold, the mountain was full of chariots of fire around Elisha.

4
Seek Ye First
the Kingdom of God

Let me tell you now about the trip the Lord sent me on to Florida.

It was mentioned at a Bible study that one of the churches had a bus going to a Christian retreat in Florida. The Lord said He wanted me to go. I prayed about it and mentioned it to my husband. Of course, I wanted him to go too. But as I prayed one night, the Lord showed me a woman with whom my husband worked who would be going with me.

I still wasn't sure I wanted to go because I was in the middle of a physical problem just like the woman who touched the hem of Jesus' robe.

Again, I prayed, "Lord, if You really want me to go, I want You to supply the exact cost of the trip."

We had been told a certain amount, and that's what I asked for. This was about ten o'clock Sunday morning. The bus was leaving one week later, and I also needed a seat to be open. By four o'clock that same day, I had the money.

Now, I had the money, but no word from Mary, the woman the Lord showed me I was to go with. Time was getting short.

One morning the Lord said to call and make my reservations. I called and talked to the pastor. I told him I was sure the Lord had another person in mind to go, but I hadn't heard anything. I mentioned her name, and he described a woman. I said, "That's her!" He said she had just made her reservation the night before! Praise God! I started preparing to go.

-·✻·-

One evening, as I was looking at a Christian magazine, it seemed as though the name of a minister and a phone number just jumped out at me from one of the pages. The Lord said, "While on your trip, I want you to call him." I wrote down the name and number and put them in my wallet so I wouldn't forget them.

-·✻·-

When we got on the bus, I was surprised to see how many people I knew. We weren't very far when the Lord spoke to me and said someone was making the trip by faith and we should take up a collection. Since I wasn't a member of this church, I thought I should speak to the pastor and ask him to pray about it.

We stayed at a motel in North Carolina. Again, the Lord brought to mind the phone number I had. I shared this with a sister in the Lord. She said to call collect. I prayed and asked for wisdom. Then I went back to my room and asked the ladies there to pray with me. We prayed and someone said, "Why don't you call collect!" So, I called collect.

The minister's wife answered. She put him on the phone, and he accepted my call.

I told him who I was, where I was going, and why I was calling. Then I felt we should pray.

As he prayed, the Lord gave me a word for him. The word in general stated that he should go into all the world and witness God's Word.

He then told me they had just started a television ministry in his church and were planning to go all over. He thanked me and that was the end of our conversation.

That week in Florida, the speaker mentioned something that was just for me. He said you never know when God will use some lady to call you from somewhere to confirm your ministry.

-·✻·-

After arriving in Florida, the pastor from the bus came to me and told me about a young man on the bus who didn't have any money and had made the trip on faith. Someone had put some money under his door. I want to thank whoever it was and pray that the Lord blesses them.

-·✻·-

I was really blessed with the way the Lord took care of my physical problem in Florida.

While I was there, I talked to the maid. She told me that some of the help were out and that her workload was extra heavy. The Lord told me to help her, so I went along and again was at my old job. I was able to pray over the rooms once more as I had done back home.

It was a beautiful trip. I was blessed so much that I didn't have time to think about my physical problem.

Coming home on the bus, our Sunday morning worship lasted for three hours. I was able to share a little about my life.

When I arrived home and my husband found out I hadn't received my healing, he said, "If you're not healed by Friday, I want you to go to the doctor."

I sort of got angry. I don't know at whom, but I started to pray. "Lord, Your Word says, 'Seek ye first the kingdom of God, and his righteousness; and all these things shall be added unto you'" (Matt. 6:33). I continued praying and talking to the Lord saying, "I even went on this trip, Lord, in the middle of this problem."

Then, in a still, small voice I heard, "You'll be healed on Thursday."

Praise the Lord, Thursday came and I was healed.

5

By My Spirit, Saith the Lord

In Matthew 25:35 the Word says, "I was in prison and you came to me" (ESV).

At a meeting I attended on a Tuesday morning, the speaker was from a prison ministry. He asked for people to help serve a pre-Christmas dinner. Again, the Lord said to go, so I put my name in.

I was a little reluctant when the time came, but everything worked out so nicely for me to go that I knew I should.

My husband drove me to where I met some people from the Tuesday morning meeting, and off we went. (I found out later that my husband used that time to buy my Christmas present.)

We had to wait in a room for the bus that would take us to the chapel. While we were there, we were searched before going in. As I was standing there, all of a sudden, fear came over me. Instantly, I rebuked it and it left.

I looked around at all the people who were going in. I noticed a young teenager. The Lord said to me, "I want you to witness to him."

Until then I had assumed that all who were there were born-again. "Why me, Lord?" I asked. But then I remembered that I was there only because the Lord had told me to go. Even before the Lord could answer I said, "I'm willing, Lord. You make the way, and I'll do it!" I didn't think any more about it.

We waited about fifteen minutes for the bus. As we were getting on, again the Lord spoke to me and told me to sit with this young man on the bus.

Quickly I reminded the Lord that I was with just enough people to sit two by two. Again, He would need to make a way.

As I walked down the aisle, a woman ahead of me who was in our group saw someone she knew who wasn't from our group. She said, "I'm going to sit here!" It was right in front of this teenager.

"Okay, I'll sit right behind you with this young man," I said.

I found out the young man was visiting with his father. Since I knew we didn't have far to go, I started to tell him about Jesus. Although it wasn't even a five-minute ride to the chapel, before we got there, he had prayed with me and asked Jesus into his heart.

I found out he had come in with a church group just so he could see his dad. I later saw him again with his dad as I served dessert. The Lord prompted me to call him by his first name. The smile I received from him and his dad was very rewarding.

As we got off the bus, the Lord said to follow one of the ladies that I had come with and sit next to her. I did, and on the other side of me was a tall lady. I said hello and asked who she was visiting. She told me she wasn't visiting anyone, that she was an inmate. Not knowing too much about the prison, I just blurted out, "I didn't know they had women prisoners here."

She answered, "They don't; I'm a transvestite."

The peace that passes all understanding is the only way I could explain what I felt as I silently said, *Lord, only You would do this to me.*

I received a reply from the Lord not to preach at him but only to show love. We chatted off and on about different things. He told me his mother was a Christian and that he was too! He also told me how he had prayed about his condition, and he felt the Lord had led him to a doctor who was going to operate on him.

I told him that as the Lord leads us, we must back up everything He tells us with the Word of God and that God calls homosexuality an abomination. Then we started singing.

As we had talked before, I noticed a pack of cigarettes. The Lord said to pray for his smoking, so I said to him, "I feel the Lord wants me to pray for your smoking." He said okay, just that easy. (The Lord was right there, preparing the way.)

So, I prayed with him, and as we sang, I noticed he had a good voice. We were being led by a group of singers from the prisons. I said to him, "Did you ever think of joining a group of singers? You have a pretty good voice!"

He replied, "Just think how much better it will be now that I won't be smoking!"

Next, the announcer asked for volunteers in the kitchen. The Lord said to go, so I did.

There really wasn't much for me to do, but I noticed two guards standing in the back. I felt I should talk to them. I asked them if they were born-again. The one man said, "Yes, about two months ago." The other said, "I'm Jewish." I quickly replied that everyone could be born-again, but I did not feel led to say anymore.

While back near the kitchen, I started talking to a young lady who was visiting her boyfriend. We talked about the Lord. All of a sudden, she started to cry and repent of some of the things in her life.

After she left, the chaplain came into the room. I witnessed to him as I was led. I remember telling him about the young man praying with me on the way in. The chaplain didn't say too much. I then went back to my seat.

I continued to talk to the man sitting next to me. He must have been about six feet, seven inches tall. He had his hair flipped up on the side, earrings, and lipstick on. He wanted me to know that he wasn't a sissy just because he dressed like that. He said that there wasn't one man in that whole place that he was afraid of.

I told him that was more of a reason that this world needed him as a man. "You need to stand up and be counted as a strong man because we certainly have enough women speaking out," I said.

As we were talking, the guards with whom I had spoken passed by. The Lord told me to go back again to the kitchen. As I walked behind them, one of the guards took out a ring of keys. He opened some doors along the way and looked in. The Lord said to me, "I want you to anoint those keys."

I laughed to myself and then, remembering Sarah laughing, quickly stopped and said, "Lord, if You can get those keys into my hands, I'll anoint them."

Then I noticed (I don't know why I didn't notice before this) that the guard I had spoken to who said he had accepted the Lord two months before looked familiar to me. I asked him if he had gone to high school where my son and daughter had gone. It turned out that he had played football with my son. I knew that his mother, whom I had met at a Bible study, was a Spirit-filled Christian. I didn't know just where this guard was in his walk with the Lord.

As we talked, I explained how the Lord speaks to us and tells us things to do, and that right then, I was to anoint his keys.

He took them from his belt without even hesitating, handed them to me, and said to go ahead. I don't think that even ten minutes had passed since the time the Lord told me to do it.

(It was only recently that I heard a testimony about a young man in a prison elsewhere who had received money that had been anointed. As he touched it, he heard himself say, "Get me the chaplain; I want to find out how to be saved!")

I prayed an anointing on the keys and handed them back. The guard told me they opened every cell in the prison.

We continued to talk, and he asked if I wasn't afraid to be there. I answered that the Bible says God puts angels around us to protect us. If the Lord told me to come there, He would protect me.

I started to go back to my seat again when the Lord spoke to me and told me to stand still. He said, "I want to show you My protection."

As I stood there, a prisoner walked toward me. As he got closer, he all of a sudden fell over and could hardly get up. I knew then that I was being watched over very carefully.

--·✤·--

The guard told me that not all the prisoners there were Christians. Some had come just for the food, but God knew the ones who needed Jesus.

As I shook hands with many of them, the Lord said, "Ask them if they know Me." So, as we stood in line shaking hands, the Lord would point some out to me. I would ask, "Do you know Jesus?"

They would look at me and say, "Yes, I do!"

The Word says in Matthew 10:32, "Whosoever therefore shall confess me before men, him will I confess also before my Father which is in heaven."

On our way out, as we were talking over some of our experiences, someone mentioned all the different crimes these men had committed. I think that was the first time I felt a little weak.

-·✻·-

My husband and I went back the next year around Christmas. We went to a Sunday morning service and sat with the prisoners. The two next to us started looking through my Bible. It was pretty new; my son, Jerry, had given it to me for my birthday. They had never seen one like it. It's called a Parallel Bible with four different translations in it. On the way in, I had taken out all the personal things I had in it but left a few teaching papers. As the men were looking at it, the Lord told me to give it to them. I did!

You should have seen the look on the one man's face. I knew there has to be a reason when the Lord tells you to do something, and you could see it in this man. He couldn't thank me enough. I even received a letter from him later thanking me again and saying how he needed the teachings that I had left in the Bible.

-·✻·-

A few years later, the Lord told me to pray in tongues for an hour from midnight to one o'clock for seven days. After praying only a few nights, we heard on the news that some of the prisoners had taken hostages and had guns. I continued to pray for seven nights.

The following morning, I woke and began to pray. I felt the Lord wanted to give me a word, and I began to write. The date was November 2, 1981. The Lord told me to look to Him that day. He wanted to bless not by might, nor by power, but by His Spirit (Zech. 4:6). He said to be willing to go when He said go. "My yoke is easy and my burden is light" (Matt. 11:30). It ended with, "Go now in peace, for the time has come."

The Lord had told me I was to march all around the prison. I said, "Lord, how can I do that?" As I sat waiting for an answer, it suddenly came to me that I could completely circle the prison in my car. So, when the Lord said the time had come, I got in my car and drove away.

I started to decide which way to go when the Lord told me to go in the opposite direction of what I was thinking. I drove all around the prison. Almost the entire time going not by what I would have done, but by how the Lord was leading.

I came to some roadblocks, but with the Lord's guidance, I did not go through any. He led me around them. Sometimes, I didn't even know where I was. I would make a turn and there right in front of me was the prison.

When I arrived at the point where I would have started, I noticed a blocked road. Only the exit lane was open. When I got back to the place where I had started, the Lord said to me, "It's finished." (I had been speaking in tongues the whole way.) I praised the Lord and went home.

That evening my husband and I picked up a friend in the Lord and went to have some hot chocolate. We turned the radio on and heard that everything had been settled that day at the prison. My husband knew about my praying for seven nights, but that was the first chance I had to share what I had done that day.

I then prayed and asked the Lord to show me what had happened that morning.

The next morning, I had a phone call from a friend and was told that the prisoner had surrendered his gun the morning I had "marched around the prison."

Praise God! "Not by might, nor by power, but by my spirit, saith the LORD of hosts" (Zech. 4:6).

6

Let the Little Children Come

Again, in Matthew 25:35-36 the Word says, "I was a stranger . . . and you clothed me" (NIV). Some dear friends of ours brought a man from India to visit us. He was speaking at their church. It was winter and his last night in our area. We had a wonderful evening of praying and sharing.

He told us the story about when he was running an orphanage in India and they didn't have any food. One of the little children said to him, "Why can't we pray for food like the Bible says!" He told us he didn't even know if he had the faith to believe, but he had to do what he had been teaching these children. So, they prayed. The next morning when they woke, they found the backyard filled with mushrooms!

When they were getting ready to leave our home and had put on their coats, the Lord spoke to me and said, "Remember that black topcoat you have in your closet? Give it to this man." (The coat had belonged to my dad who had passed away.) I first thought, "But Lord, he has a coat," but I got it anyway. I said to him, "I hope you're not offended, but the Lord told me to give you this coat."

He looked at me and reached out his hand to take it. "I do not have a coat," he said. "This one I have on is borrowed!"

--❄--

One day as I was reading a verse in Romans, I prayed and asked the Lord to reveal it to me. I read and prayed for about two hours. Nothing came. I prayed and prayed for wisdom, when suddenly the Lord said, "I want you to relax."

I eagerly got up from the table, laid down on the sofa, and closed my eyes. I thought, *Thanks, Lord. That's a very good idea.*

As soon as I closed my eyes, I had a vision. I saw a little girl. She had a very long letter in her hands. I looked at how young she was and said, "Lord, that girl is too little to read that big letter."

In my vision I saw the Lord nodding His head yes. I knew He was telling me that no matter how much wisdom I prayed for, I was just not able to understand that Scripture at this time.

I told this to a friend in the Lord and was given this Scripture in John 16:12, "I have yet many things to say unto you, but ye cannot hear them now." *The Living Bible* says, "you can't understand them now."

-·�֍·-

There are times when the Lord has me call a counseling center and pray with someone there. There is one dear sister especially whom I have called. She has said that it is always when she has a need.

One time I called the center and a woman answered. I told her the Lord told me to call and pray for whoever answered. He said to pray for her ear. She said she almost turned back and went home but decided not to and that this was only her second call, so we were both praising the Lord!

-·✖·-

In our home we have a room which we call our prayer room. When we built our home, it was on the plans as a garage. We decided to make it a prayer room instead. We put a closet in it and then found out that our oil tank had to go in it too. After all was done, the space left open was exactly ten percent of the area of the whole house. Praise God! We even got to tithe our home!

Many prayers have been said in that room. A friend of ours prayed with one of my husband's bosses there. He asked Jesus into his heart and spoke in tongues the same night. He had been down, and my husband had witnessed to him at work.

A little later we were at a meeting together where words of prophecy were coming forth. I felt this man had a word to give, but nothing came forth. After the meeting I said to him, "Did you know that you had a word to give?" He said he had one sentence that he knew the Lord was saying, but he couldn't give it. He thanked me for confirming that it was from God.

A year after he had received the Lord, we were praying in the prayer room as the Lord led us when we had guests. This same man gave his first word of prophecy there.

-·✳·-

One Sunday morning, right after we had built our home, I was getting company for dinner, but I said to my husband, "I don't care what I have to do, I'm taking time to pray and sit with the Lord." He said okay but did not offer to come along with me to the prayer room.

I got my Bible and went and sat there feeling really good that I had made the decision to give that time to the Lord. As I sat there in prayer, the Lord spoke to me and said, "This is very nice that you are giving Me this time, but your husband is upstairs, doing your dishes!" I knew instantly which one of us was giving our time to the Lord in the way He wanted it then! The Lord's way is doing what His Word would have us do and getting our priorities in order.

-·�֍·-

I remember one time when my mom and grandmom were visiting. Each morning, I had tried to give my first awakening moments to the Lord, but while they were there, I had to jump right out of bed and do something for my grandmother. I thought, "Lord, I'm sorry I can't give You those first minutes." He spoke to me and said, "Don't you realize that you are giving them to Me in action as you jump out of bed to help your grandmother?"

Those quiet times are important, but I find that the Lord calls us to be a Martha as well as a Mary!

-·✖·-

We have a young friend who had been in an accident and had a miracle in his life. Many people had prayed for him. The Lord led me to pray in tongues for him whenever he came to mind.

One evening as I prayed, I jumped out of bed and started to write. It was a word for this young man. One of the things mentioned was that he would be blessed financially and he would bless others. A few weeks later, he received a very large sum of money. Praise God!

Jeremiah 33:3 tells us the Lod will "shew thee great and mighty things, which thou knowest not." Revelation 1:1 says that God through Jesus Christ, gave His servants revelations of things that must come to pass.

-·✳·-

One day while my husband was at work, he was witnessing and sharing with some men. A man who had been living on a mountain near here with a guru as his leader came over to them and heard my husband telling of something that the Lord had done in my life. He said, "Would you ask if she would pray for a girl I know who's dying of bone cancer?"

My husband and I started praying for her. While at our Tuesday night Bible study which we attend weekly, I received a word from the Lord that I should be anointed for her. "And I sought for a man among them, that should make up the hedge, and stand in the gap before me for the land" (Ezek. 22:30). I stood for her in the group and was anointed for her.

In a little while this man came to my husband and told him she had been ninety percent healed. We both agreed that the Lord does not heal only ninety percent, and we stood on the Word for a complete healing. The man came back again and said she went to a hospital in New York and had a bone biopsy. She was completely healed. Praise the Lord!

7

That They Might Have Abundant Life

Now ladies, even when we go to our little gatherings called demonstrations or home parties, God has surprises for us.

I attended a plant demonstration one evening at my neighbor's. To my surprise, the Lord told me to pray with the demonstrator. I waited until all had left and asked her if she needed prayer for anything. She said she was born-again, but she was having problems at home. I prayed with her that night. About a year later I met her and her husband at a Bible study. They were both walking with the Lord.

Another time I was at a Tupperware party when the Lord told me this demonstrator was ready to ask Him into her heart. This was at my niece's home. The demonstrator was a school friend of hers. I didn't pray with her that night, but I asked the Lord for another time. The day she brought the orders, I had to run my money up to my niece's home. That was when her friend asked Jesus into her heart.

I didn't hear from her for quite a while, but when we met again at my niece's and shared it was great to see how much she had grown in the Lord in that time. We started going to a Bible study together. Within a few weeks, her husband accepted Jesus. She also has a neighbor who reads the Koran and sees all these things happening in this girl's life. She has been watching some Christian TV shows and asking a lot of questions. Praise God!

When my niece moved up the road from us, she told me later she thought I was a little off. But as I gave her the Word, she tried to disprove me by studying it herself. She had accepted the Lord when she was younger! She has grown in leaps and bounds in the Lord, and her husband also has accepted Jesus into his heart. Praise the Lord!

- · ✻ · -

Have you ever had an obscene phone call? I was as surprised as you. I witnessed about this at one meeting. Afterwards, a young lady came over to me and said she had one. She wanted to tell the caller about Jesus, but nothing would come out of her mouth. So, she prayed that God would have him call someone who would witness to him. She was really glad to hear my testimony. We had the same telephone office.

At first, I was shocked when I received the call. I didn't even know what the man was saying. When I heard the Lord tell me what it was, I knew that God loved him and I told him so.

He prayed with me and asked Jesus into his heart. I told him to get involved in a Bible-believing church and mentioned one to him. I said there were new people coming in all the time.

My son was with me at the time. When I hung up the phone, he said to me, "Was that what I think it was?"

-·✳·-

In the past seven years, the Lord has led me in many directions. I have led about sixty-five people to ask Jesus into their hearts (on a one-to-one basis) including a priest, a nun, a ninety-two-year-old woman, a young child, many relatives, and even neighbors. Some were people I knew, and some were people I only met once. Someone else had sown the seed, and the Lord just had me pray with them.

I do volunteer work at a local hospital where I have seen many prayers answered and some that weren't. (Maybe one day I can write more details on this.) I also volunteer once a month at a state mental hospital. But ladies, with all this, first of all I am a wife, mother, and grandmother; and I'm not too busy to enjoy all these roles. I very seldom go out in the evening to any meetings without my husband, so we have a lot of time together.

My children come to Sunday dinner, and sometimes my daughter brings the kids for lunch. Hardly a day goes by when I don't see them.

Hallelujah! Put God first in your life and He orders your steps (Ps. 37:23), and they are just where you want to go too.

Many of my days are spent visiting the elderly. So many of them have prayed with me and asked Jesus into their hearts!

One time, my husband and I were at a prayer meeting where they had prayed for a young lady in a wheelchair. The Lord spoke to me later and said we were to go pray with her. I told Jerry and he agreed to go. We said a little prayer with her. After we prayed, she said she had asked God to send someone to her to confirm something for her. We know we're going to see her walking, and we love the times we have spent together. She has been a big part of our lives.

Daily the Lord looks for someone to stay in the gap, to reach out and pray. I pray that after reading this and seeing the different ways God can use us for His glory, just in our daily lives, you also will be willing to be that person.

Family Scriptures

Jeremiah 32:39 – I will give them one heart, and one way, that they may fear me for ever, for the good of them, and of their children after them.

Psalm 115:14 – The LORD shall increase you more and more, you and your children.

Proverbs 20:7 – The just man walketh in his integrity: his children are blessed after him.

Proverbs 14:26 – In the fear of the LORD is strong confidence: and his children shall have a place of refuge.

Proverbs 22:6 – Train up a child in the way he should go: and when he is old, he will not depart from it.

Psalm 128:1, 3 – Blessed is every one that feareth the LORD; that walketh in his ways. Thy wife shall be as a fruitful vine by the sides of thine house: thy children like olive plants round about thy table.

Genesis 7:1 – Come thou and all thy house into the ark.

Psalm 37:26 – He is ever merciful, and lendeth; and his seed is blessed.

Psalm 102:28 – The children of thy servants shall continue, and their seed shall be established before thee.

The Sinner's Prayer

"I tell you the truth, unless you are born again,
you cannot see the Kingdom of God."
John 3:3 NLT

If you want to know that you know God, say this little prayer:

Jesus, I believe You died on the cross for my sins. Forgive me for those sins and come into my heart.

www.ingramcontent.com/pod-product-compliance
Lightning Source LLC
Chambersburg PA
CBHW070800050426
42452CB00012B/2428